9/24

THE SECR

HISTORY

OF

PYTHAGORAS.

Translated from the
ORIGINAL COPY,
Lately found at
OTRANTO in ITALY

by

Samuel Croxall

'Αθανάτυς μὲν πρῶτα Θεὺς, νόμῳ ὡς διάκειἶαι
Τιμᾶ. ——————   Pyth. Carm. Aur.

THE PREFACE.

THE Translation of this venerable Piece of Antiquity is undertook upon a double Score; being designed as well to entertain the Curiosity of the Learned, as to supply the Defects of the Ignorant. If the original Language would have been more acceptable to the one, it would have been less intelligible to the other. I cannot, without uttering a Falsity, venture to affirm that so singular and valuable a Piece will be made Public, at least as yet: And in the mean Time I shall flatter myself, that this little Essay may contribute in some sort or other to the diversion, if not Instruction, of People in every Condition of Life.

If this is well received, the other Parts will make their Appearance at proper Distances of Time. I publish no more at present, because I would not be thought to impose too much upon any one's Patience; as for losing my own Labour, I am under no bad Apprehensions about that; for the Reader cannot reject with a greater Disdain, than I have translated with Pleasure, the Contents of this Book.

I shall say little by way of Apology for the Subject Matter of it, since it is not my Business to think it wants any, and the Nature of the Thing speaks so amply for itself. That Pythagoras, who held the Transmigration of Souls, pretended to remember things transacted in the bodies which he had formerly animated, has been universally allowed. Ovid in the fifteenth Book of his Metamorphoses, introduces him in a Lecture to his Disciples, saying thus of himself:

Ipse Ego (nam memini) Trojani tempore belli
Panthoides Euphorbus eram, &c.

and he proceeds to mention some Particulars which happened to him at that Time. Why therefore may he not as well be supposed to have recorded the great Variety of Incidents which he must have met with in the other Bodies which he inhabited? One would almost suspect that Ovid had seen the following Memoirs, and taken his Hints from them; since he makes our Philosophers, speaking of the Depravity of Mankind, say

Ipsos Inscripsere Deos sceleri, Numenque supernum
Cœde laboriseri credunt gaudere juvenci.

But there is no Room to question it, when presently after we find he puts these Words into his Mouth;

O Gemis attonitum gelidæ formidine mortis !
Quid Styga, quid tenebras, quid nomina vana
Materiem Vatum?   [timetis,

So little Reason is there for being surprised at the Revival of this History now, that we might be reckoned strangely insipid, if we had not concluded there had once been such a Thing extant, though it had utterly perished among the Ruins of Time.

The Greek Sentence which I have put in the Title-Page for a Motto,

Ἀθανάτυς μὲν πρῶτα Θεὺς, νόμῳ ὡς διάκειλαι
Τιμᾷ. ——————   Pyth. Carm. Aur.

and which is Pythagoras his own, being the Beginning of his Golden Verses, seems to be a Precept which he would have us think he had been taught in the Person of Æthalides; for it is in English,

Worship the immortal Gods as by Law established.

Human Laws respecting altogether the external Behaviour and Deportment, and not being capable in their Nature of affecting the Heart; this Philosopher takes Occasion more than once to excite us to an Observance of them. The Laws of God, which also regard the inward Regulation of the Mind, and are not of a Quality to fall under the Cognizance of human Judges, he refers to the Arbitation of Reason; and questions not, if we are determined by that, but they will meet with a ready Compliance.

If anyone, to show his Skill in Criticism, should remark that this Secret History, because of the Inaccuracy and Uncertainty of its Style, does not seem to have been compiled by so learned a Philosopher: I have one Thing to observe to him, which ought in Reason to out-balance all the Occasions for Cavil upon that Account; he is not to look upon this as a regular Performance, but as what undoubtedly it was, Minutes taken in Short-Hand by some Symposiac or Disciple, and filled up afterwards, upon a leisurely Recollection.

Besides, as the shortness of a Prospect is sometimes thought to be a Disadvantage to it, so possibly this may be the less pleasing upon the same Account. Therefore I am to acquaint the Reader, that the whole Vista will be opened by Degrees, which I hope will be the more surprising: Brown Shades, and flowry Meadows, the winding Stream, and the old Ruins, the diftant Woods gilded with Sunshine, and beyond all, the blueish Mountains, will successively appear. I have given no more here than what may be seen without {training the Sight, or ascending an Eminence; it is not designed to take off the Eye from Things of greater Consequence, but may be perused at the Repast of the Tea-Table, or in a Coffee-House Vacation.

INTRODUCTION.

SINCE the Learned are already sufficiently apprised, by their respective Correspondents from Italy, of the great Treasure of Curiosities which has been lately discovered there in the Garden of an ancient Palace, which slands upon the Ruins of the old Town of Croton, I shall detain the Reader no longer with a particular Account of that Matter, than what is just necessary to illustrate the Subject I am going to communicate.

In a Part of the Wilderness belonging to the Gardens of a decayed Palace of a certain Cardinal, near Otranto, there has been, for some Generations past, a large Cascade almost naturally formed, which falls down the Sides of a broken Rock into a Basin of no small Circumference; in which, for Want of due Inspection and Repair, (the Cardinal residing mostly at another Palace situated more conveniently in Respect to its Distance from Rome) there has been, long since, a Rupture, or Chasm on one Side near the Bottom; at which the Water having, for some Time, emptied itself, did, at last, so dilute and wash away the concrete Particles of which the Cement consisted, which held the Stones of the Foundation together, that the whole Fabric sunk in one Night. The Depth of this Sinking made those who saw it the next Day, apprehend it to have been the Effects of an Earthquake; till, being searched into not long after, by some Workmen who were set to repair it, it was discovered to be caused by the falling in of an Arch, over which the Basin was built. This Arch, by the Fragments of it, appeared to have been designed for the Roof or Covering of some Grotto; and, from the Pieces of Carving, still remaining upon it, some of the more curious Spectators concluded it to be antique.

Upon clearing the Place of its Rubbish, they were soon, to their great Satisfaction, confirmed in their Opinion. For the whole was found to be a handsome large Room, near upon square, about forty Foot over each way, and as many in Height. The Door or Entrance near thirty Foot high, with a Window on each side it, which were all the Lights it had, made this Front of the Building look very spacious and grand; which yet altogether was plain, and of the Doric Order. Within were several Niches properly disposed, each containing a very fair Bust of Parian Marble, and the Pedestal of Egyptian. I am told that several Medals were dug up under the Pavement, which consisted of very thick hard red Tiles, about eight Inches square. An Account, of all which, and many other Antiquities equally entertaining, will soon be published in a Discourfe or Treatise purposely written by the Learned Signor Florentini the Pope's Librarian; who was sent thither by his Holiness, at the Request of the Cardinal, with a special Commission to take; the Care and Cognizance of them.

Therefore, to come to our present Purpose; I must inform the World, that a hopeful young Gentleman, Son to a most ingenious and obliging Friend of mine, happening in the Course of his Travels to Jye at an Inn in the Neighbourhood of this Place, the third Night after the Discovery was made, stayed there five Days; hoping, by indefatigable Industry and Application, to make himself Master of some little Piece of these Antiquities; having a good Relish and Judgment for Things of that Kind.

But Orders being sent from Rome, from the Cardinal, that a Guard should be set near the Place, and all Persons whatever strictly kept off from Approaching it, he had but a faint Prospect of accomplishing his Wishes: Till one Evening, as he was walking out after Sun-set, he met a poor Labourer with a Spade and Mattock on his Shoulder, returning from his Work. The young Gentleman, letting slip no Opportunity of exercising himself in the Italian Tongue, which the ordinary Peasant there (quite contrary to what happens in most other Countries) speaks as properly as the best bred Courtier at Rome, took occasion to enter upon Discourse with him; and soon with a secret Pleasure found, that the Conversation he held was with one of those who were employed in clearing away the Rubbish of the Ruins in the Cardinal's Garden.

Fired with fresh Expeditions upon so welcome an Interview, he first warily founded the poor Man's Capacity, hoping he might find him one of those experienced Pioneers, who knew how to turn such sort of Work in some Measure to their own Advantage; and from whom, most of the late-found Medals and Antiquities which have been brought from Italy; have, by clandestine Practices, been obtained. In fine, this Rustic, as simple as he appeared, was one of these; and having taken his Opportunity to conceal something which he thought might be of Value, he afterwards, under Pretence of going to drink at a little Fountain, which gushed out of 2 Lyon's Head, fixed in the Garden Walk threw his Prize unseen into an adjoining Meadow; from whence he had been to fetch it just as the young Traveller met him.

These two had very luckily happened upon each other, being the properest Persons they could mutually communicate their Designs to: For whenever any curious Thing of Value or Antiquity is procured by any Stranger, unless he uses the utmost Precaution in conveying it out of the Country, he is sure to have it seized and taken from him; nay, though he has paid ever so fair a Price for it, and purchased it of the rightful Proprietor.

To be short; the poor Peasant having a just Confidence in the young Gentleman, without Hesitation drew out from under his Cloths a Cylinder of about a Foot long, and five Inches Diameter. It was caked over with a rough Case of Earth and Rust intermingled; and by its Lightness seemed to be hollow; which attempting with a Knife, they were soon certified of; for they found it very thin, and made shift to raise up, and separate one

End, as one would open the Head of an Oyster-Barrel. There appeared to be nothing in it but a Roll of Parchment or Vellum, curiously rolled round a small Stick of black Ebony, at each End of which was a little Boss of white Cornelian. Our young Virtuoso, without staying to examine the Contents, made it his own for five Crowns, and deferred the Perusal of it to a more proper Time and Place.

This Volume, since the young Gentle man, Return, by the very obliging and communicative Temper of his Father, is now in my Hands; and I have a Permission from both to publish such an Account of it as I shall think proper; which now the Reader may prepare himself for, and is as follows.

The Writing is in the Greek Tongue, of an ancient fair Character; but the Ink so decayed and faded by Time, that at present it is barely legible, and no more. I have transcribed it with the utmost Care and Exactness; and can aver, that I solemnly believe I have not omitted or mistaken one Letter.

On the outside of the Roll was written *Codex Pompilianus*; meaning, that the Book had belonged to *Numa Pompilius*, the second King of Rome, which is most probable; or to some other Roman of that Name. On the inside was the Title:

Τὰ Πυθαγόρε τῦ τῆς Σοφίας φίλε ἀπόῤῥηία

The secret History of Pythagoras the Philosopher

As indeed it has been hitherto. For though Men of Learning have all along been acquainted with that great Man's Notions of the Transmigration of the Soul, which he used to assert from his own particular Experience; professing that his had belonged first of all to the Body of Æthalides, then to those of Euphorbus, Hermotimus, and Pyrrhus a poor Fisherman of Delos, successively; yet they never were informed sufficiently of such co-temporary Circumstances and Parts of History, as the Mind of one so observant upon all remarkable Passages must needs have collected, in the different Bodies or Stages of Life in which it resided. These are the Contents of this *Pompilian* Volume; which seems to have been in the keeping of some noble Inhabitant of Croton; though it is not impossible but Numa himself might have had a House there. How long it has been thus lost to the World, or whether indeed it were ever publicly known to it, cannot; I think, easily be determined. It was found under the Pavement, as if designedly laid there; either before the Building was erected, or to be concealed upon some Emergency which happened after. Possibly upon that Irruption which the Gauls made into Italy, under their King Brennus, when they over-ran all before them, and plundered even Rome itself. For there being scarce anything extant of the Romans till after that Time, in which we could expect any mention of Pythagoras's Works, makes it not unlikely that this was the only Book of that kind in being; and by the unhappy Care of its Professor, who might fall in that Time of Calamity, came to be buried in so long an Obscurity.

The Use I shall put it to at present, till the present Proprietor resolves to make the Original public, is to communicate to the World the Contents of it in a Translation into our own Tongue; which I intend to serve up, to, keep the Appetites of my Readers from being cloyed, in moderate Parcels; that the Whole may last the longer, and that proper Portions of it may be set before them from time to time as their Stomachs may seem to call for it.

MEMOIR I.
The History of ÆTHALIDES.

MY Mother's Name was Melidora; she lived in the Suburbs of Paphos, in the Island of Cyprus; and procured herself an honest unenvied Livelihood, by furnishing several of its Inhabitants with Milk, Honey, and all Sorts of delicious Fruits as the Season required. She rented a little Farm and Garden of a Merchant in the City, as her Mother had done before her; from whence she provided many Conveniences for the Citizens, a comfortable Maintenance for herself, and a handsome Education for me. For she sent me to the principal School in the Town; where I was instructed among the Children of People of the first Rank, in all the Sciences that are proper to adorn a Man, and make him useful to his Country.

As my Age came on, my Love of Knowledge increased; and notwithstanding the great Care of my Matter, and tender Fondness of my Mother, who were daily feeding my Mind with all the Notions that were adapted to cherish and improve it, I continually gave Instances of so inquisitive a Temper, as rather afforded Pleasure than Trouble to those about me.

One Day, perceiving I was without a Father, a Happiness I could not see, without repining, in some of my Equals, I enquired of my Mother concerning it, with more than usual Importunity. Young as I was, I could not help observing the sudden Blush which overspread her beautiful Neck and Face at this Question. She was not then above One and Twenty; and as I have since heard from many Reports, did not yield to the fairest Woman in that City for the Charms of her Person. She strained me in her Arms with much Rapture, and after having overwhelmed me with with a thousand kisses: yes, my dearest Æthalides (says she) I will tell you; and that which has been the Cause of your present Being, and will be the Means of your future Welfare, shall no longer be kept secret from you.

Know then, my dearest Child, pursued she, that I was scarce thirteen Years old, when in the Evening of a hot Summer's Day, I chanced to fall asleep under the Hedge of Roses, which grows on the side of the little Rivulet, which runs through our Garden. My Mother not being yet returned from the Town, whither her Business had carried her, and the Servants employed in some more remote Part of the Garden, I lay thus till the Dusk of the Night was far advanced. The Freshness of the cool Breezes, and the Stillness of the Place, which was rendered more agreeable by the warbling Notes of corresponding Nightingales, contributed so irresistibly to tie down my Senses with the silken Cords of Morpheus, that I did not awake before I found myself irrecoverably within the Arms and Power of a most beautiful young Man. I would have employed my Strength in Resistance, but the sudden Surprise had deprived me of it; I would have raised my Voice for Help, but Fear had disarmed my Tongue: And the Attention, which I could not avoid giving to an Accident so new to me, conspired to complete my Undoing. For whether Love had so early begun to find the way to my Heart, or whether it was only a Childish Prelude to it, the Features of this Person so resembled those of a handsome Youth of Paphos, whom I had eagerly gazed at the Day before, when he came to our House (as he frequently did) to buy Fruits, that, notwithstanding the

Anguish I ought to have felt upon such an Occasion, by that fatal Prepossession of my Fancy, I was all over melted into Tenderness. There was nothing to restrain him from indulging the Warmth of his Passion to the last Degree of Desire, but the eternal and unalterable Rules of Nature; which at length, after repeated Instances of his first Provocation, consented to free me from his Embraces. By this time my Senses, having re-assembled themselves to condole with me upon this Violation of my Honour, plunged me into an inexpressible Sorrow. I lay still on the Ground, and I question whether my Grief would ever have suffered me to rise, if the charming Ravisher had not gently lifted me up.

After having folded me in his Arms with a forcible Transport, he addressed himself thus to me, in the sweetest Accents that ever my Ears were blessed withal. "Farewell, my lovely Melidora, and to calm all your Troubles, remember that that the Son of Jove was the Author of them. Yes, most amiable Nymph, it is Hermes, who has this Night improved his Immortality in your Fruition; who has assumed the Person of Neanthus, "the Son of Chrysander, to gain the easier Admittance to your Heart; and in his Shape will continue to perform the kind Offices due to you and your Offspring all the Days of your Lives." He had scarce said these Words, when the Voices of the Servants, who had been searching for me all over the Garden, reached our Ears, upon which the God your Father, unwilling to make any Discovery to my Prejudice, flew to the little Wicket in the Wall, and unlocked it with as much Dexterity, as if he had had the real Key. And that Neanthus, our Landlord the Merchant's Son, who is so fond of you, and whose Presence so often blesses this Roof, is indeed nothing less than what he seems to be, but the artful Son of the Thunderer, who retains the Form of that Son of Chrysander, which was long since shipwrecked near the Island of Rhodes, that he may the more favourably continue to his helpless Dependants the Protection, which by his Means is become so necessary to them. She finished her Discourse with giving me a Charge of the strictest Secrecy, which for my Part I kept inviolably; but the whimsical Conditions of my half Immortality after Death being published to the World, gave undoubted Tokens of my heavenly Extraction. If the Happiness of being let into such a Secret had made the Head of giddy Childhood swim with Vanity, it would not have been unpardonable; but it had not that Erred upon me. Indeed it darted a most exquisite Pleasure into my Heart, and elevated all my Senses with gentle Ebulitions of Joy. When I reflected upon my Birth, it swelled my Mind with an Ambition to be worthy of it, without infusing into me the least Tincture of Pride. I had been early instructed in the Principles of Religion and Morality; and Eleutherius my Master, that I might have a just Notion of the Gods, had taken care first to make me understand their Attributes, that I might not entertain any absurd or contradictory Opinions concerning their Nature.

All the Inhabitants of Foreign Nations (says he) and the Generality of our own People are educated in false Principles of Religion, the better to serve the Interests and Designs of cheating Priests, who are so well skilled in these kind of Artifices, that they know no Basis so proper to build their Tyranny upon, as an established Ignorance. The better to support and cherish this, they provide that Mankind should be trained up from their early Childhood, when, like Wax, they are softest and fittest to take Impressions, in such wrong mistaken Notions of the Deity, as may be most subservient to their Purposes, This fine Scheme takes place before they can well speak, and they are taught what they must believe of the Gods, before they are capable of knowing them or anything else. All the Ideas they are made to conceive of them are such as belong to Men only; that they are passionate, revengeful, partial, jealous, vain-glorious, resolving, repenting, mistaken, that they are circumscribed in their Actions by Time and Place, sometimes pleased, and sometimes displeased; whereas in Truth, my dearest Child, there is one only real and very God, who ordained all Things, and on whom all Things depend; and the several Gods and Goddesses, with so many several Names which the Vulgar are taught to worship, are indeed no more than so many several Attributes and Qualities of this true God.

With him, my Æthalides, I must make you well acquainted: To which, there is no more requisite, than that you should form a right Conception of his Attributes. Take care that these may be always such as are consistent with, and agreeable to, the Nature of him that made the Universe, and keeps it in so continued an Order. Consider, that to do this, he must be Allwise, and All-powerful, Infinite, Immutable and Eternal; and so absolutely Perfect in all Respects, that neither his Wisdom nor his Power, his Goodness nor his Happiness, are capable of any Addition or Diminution.

When you are convinced of this, (as your Reason will readily convince you of it) you can never suffer yourself to think, with the Vulgar, that a Deity absolutely perfect is liable to the Passions and Imperfections of us poor Mortals. Can you suppose him angry, or grieved, or jealous, without implying a Diminution of his Happiness? Can you conceive Him upon any account partial, who is infinitely just? Can a Being, All-wise, and Good, without great Absurdity, be represented Vain glorious, making Resolutions, and repenting of them, and sometimes mistaken? Can He be All-powerful, and yet be imagined to want Time to complete his Work, and to fail in many of his Attempts? How gross is the Idea of His being more in one part of Space than another, when compared with his Infinity? How wretchedly stupid, those of His being passionate and revengeful, when we reflect: upon his Immutability and great Perfection? Yet thus foolish, thus absurd, thus ignorantly profane is the poor deluded Multitude by the Impositions of misrepresenting Priests. The Men of this Profession make the credulous People believe that they converse with the Gods with much Familiarity, and have a very good Interest with, and Influence over, them: That they can prevail with them to do this, or to desist from that, that, just as they please; and to send Good or Evil among Mankind, according as they shall represent Matters to them. When they think themselves not treated with sufficient Respect, they say, that the Gods are angry, and threaten the World with nothing less than Plague or Famine to revenge the Affront, God, my dearest Æthatides, is indeed the Author of all Things, since nothing can be done without him; and consequently Plagues and Famines happen as he appoints: But I think the shallow Knowledge of Man has no Warrant to determine, whether they are sent as Judgments or not. The World was always too full of Wickedness not to deserve Punishment: But thinkest thou, Æthalides, that the raging Pestilence which last Year swept away almost the whole City of Athens, fell upon the most wicked Spot of all the Earth; or that the Gods designed to show their Justice, when Aristus, Philaretes and Polimedon fell undistinguished in the Infection, and Laolestes, Autophilus and Misander escaped? No certainly: For Athens yielded to no City in the World for Politeness and Religion; and Aristus, Philaretes and Polimedon were as much esteemed for their exalted Virtues, as Laolestes, Artophilus and Misander were detestable for their flagitious Enormities.

When therefore we see Men of such different Characters, whose Actions were as opposite as Light and Darkness, shot promiscuously with the Arrows of Death, tho' we can't deny it to be the Hand of God, it is shocking to call it his Vengeance, his Resentment, his Anger, his Wrath, his Fury, and those Expressions which give us such Ideas of his being peevish and implacable. How is it possible to think worthily and truly of Him who is infinitely Good, without always representing Him to our Minds as full of Love, Benevolence, Sweetness, Candour and Compassion? Have we lived in a Pursuit of Virtue and honourable Courses, and do we expect to be admitted into Elysium after Death? If We do, then how can we be insensible of the great Good-will of Jove, who sends his Messenger Death to bid us leave off Labour and go to Rest? How very benevolent and compassionate is he to the Survivors, when he is so kind as to take off the Injurious and the Oppressor, the lying Hypocrite and the crafty Knave? Nay, how very good to these Criminals themselves, when by intercepting them in the midst of their Villainies, he renders them capable of a milder Sentence from the infernal Judges? O Jove, thy Love is continual and thy Goodness unbounded! If we do our hearty Endeavour to be good like Thee, and obey those Precepts of Virtue which Thou hast written in our Mind, we are sure thou wilt not hurt us, but command the Gates of Elysium to be opened for our Reception, where we may be mingled with the Company of our virtuous honest Ancestors, and enjoy eternal Peace and Pleasure in those Fields of Joy, and Groves of Delight: But if we act contrary to that Sense of Thee which our Reason dictates to us; 'tis not a Deluge of Water, or a parched sunburned Earth, the momentary Alarms of Famine, Pestilence, or the Sword, that we ought to fear, but an Eternity of Torments under the Hands of indefatigable Furies in Hell. Thou art immutable; and so far is the presumptuous Priest from being able to change thy Decrees, which are founded upon infinite Justice, that it would be the highest Impiety to suppose Thy Nature capable of it: No: Thou art just and true in all thy Actions, and it is sufficient that we know our Doom hereafter depends upon our Actions here, without thy being represented in Statues of Wood and Stone, with Arrows and Thunderbolts listed up at our Heads, as if thou were an angry and ill-natured God.

Wherefore, my Æthalides, (continued he) keep a strict Guard over thy Mind, that thou conceivest not any Thought of the supreme Being, which is not agreeable to his Attributes; nor let the Examples of others, who entertain such strange ridiculous Fancies about him, give any Bias to thy Judgment; for thou knowest how apt the Multitude is to run into and persevere in a wrong Opinion. Do they not believe that the Sun, Moon and Stars are no bigger than they seem? that the bright Luminary of the Day falls into the Sea at Night, and rises out of it in the Morning; and that he is carried in a Chariot round this dirty Spot on which we live? Are there not some superstitious Strangers among us, which in habit somewhere near the Confines of Assyria, who boast that this luminous Orb once stopped in his full Career for some Hours, to answer the Design of a certain Mortal? Is not Jove himself wickedly supposed to have bid him lie still for three Nights together, that he might have the longer time to revel in the Arms of *Alcmena*? Whereas Thou hast been taught, that this Globe of Light is at too great a Distance from us to perform such a Rotation in a thousand million of Years; tho' it were to move as swift as the Arrows of Hercules. But the wicked Priests, my Æthalides, invent these Fables, to support their Dignity, and augment their Gains. What God, thinkest Thou, must he be, who our Priests tell us is out of humour, and discontented without a Multitude of Offerings and Sacrifices? a Man of such a Temper would be accounted covetous, and greedy, and unreasonable. What Idea canst thou have of a God who loves to regale his Nose with roasted Bullocks, and carbonaded Sheep and Goats, and Libations of rich Wine? a Man with an Appetite so continually disposed would be accounted a Glutton. But what is the God that these Offerings are served up to? Why perhaps a

Piece of Wood, or Stone, or Brass, or some such Material; carved sometimes in a very ridiculous Shape, like a Man, or a Woman, or Monster with three Heads, as Diana is represented: They have Faces and Mouths, but can neither see nor eat; they have Hands and Feet, and yet some times fall down, and are broken in pieces. Who therefore eats the roasted Beef, and the broiled Cutlets of Mutton; but the hungry voracious Priest? Who empties the smiling Goblet of its sparkling Wine, but the thirsty tippling Priest? Who says the Gods are yet displeased, and require more Offerings? the artful Priest: raising Contributions to enhance his own Dignity, from the idle Superstitions and groundless Fears of the giddy Multitude. These, my Æthalides, consider as Men exercising a Trade, to which they are educated, and by which they must live. Take care that thou affront not their Persons, nor openly ridicule their employment, for in so doing thou mayst offend and provoke the State, which for politic Ends did first institute, and for the same will continue to protest the Men of this Profession. Thou mayst laugh in private at all the Absurdities which they make the People swallow, and at the Vain Alarms by which they govern their Hopes and Fears: But beware how thou disturb or meddle with them in public for they will echo their Resentments against thee from Temple to Temple, like a Nest of Hornets provoked in the hollow Rock, and wound thy good Name with the Stings of poisonous Language.

Yet let that Virtue, by which Thou art bound to serve thy Country, exhort thee to use the Power of thy Station, whatever it be, to check their Pride and control their Ambition. Tho' they were originally designed for Servants and Instruments of the Government, yet are they very inclinable to usurp an Authority and Dominion of their own, and to tyrannize over the very Magistrate, who constitutes and appoints them. Therefore, be assured, it is the Interest of all honest Men, and Lovers of their

Country, to keep down the aspiring haughty Aims of these Cooks of State, these venerable Butchers; and never trust them with any Power, but what they will readily acknowledge to be conferred upon them by the Magistrate, in a limited Sense, for the good of the Public.

With this View were the different Ritual, and Modes of Worship first established in all the Nations and Cities round about us; each following that way which was most suitable to their Genius, and most conveniently adapted to correspond with their Form of Government. Thus *Crete* thinking itself holy above all Lands for the Story of Jupiter's being born, educated, and buried there, worships him chiefly; and looks down with Scorn and Contempt upon other Nations, as People destitute of equal Privileges, if not quite excluded from the divine Favour. But, Æthalides, canst thou help smiling at their Superstition, or dost thou pity their Stupidity and Credulity? who can be made to believe that Jove was born as we Men are; and that he was brought thither to be educated privately, lest his Father Saturn should find him and eat him? Nay, they say too, that after he had lived his Term of Life out, he died and was buried there; and they think all those very profane and wicked People, who will not believe this Nonsense, these Impossibilities.

It is probable, my Æthalides, there might have been such a Man as Jupiter, who by some extraordinary Occurrences in his Life, since improved by fabulous Traditions, may appear a very extraordinary Person, and even an Object of Worship to a superstitious bigotted World; whose natural Fears are easily wrought upon by the Stratagems of Priests, especially when they are countenanced and authorized by the Magistrate. But to esteem such a one the great Creator: and Arbiter of the Universe, (who must have existed, in the highest Perfection of everything that is good, from all Eternity) is the Effect of Ignorance, Superstition, and a blind Reliance upon old Wives Stories, and the cunning Management and Policy of Priests.

Who, but a most besotted silly People, could suppose a Being of so exalted and refined a Nature, as the high God must be, capable of having carnal Copulation with mortal Women; and filling Heaven with his his natural Offspring? One of these is the principal Object of religious Worship in the Island of Delos; another in the City of Ephesus. Bacchus is honoured in Carousels of Wine of his own Institution at Thebes; and Venus the Goddess of Love and Beauty is adored here in Cyprus. If I could enumerate all the Religions of the Earth with the Superstitions that attend them, it would only be giving you a Detail of the several Follies of credulous Mankind, and the politic Contrivances of States and Governments. The bare mentioning of these may suffice to give you a Taste of their Impostures; tho' however monstrous and absurd they appear, remember to speak of them in public with a seeming Deference and Regard, and where it is expected you should be particular in declaring for that sort of Worship which you most approve, you should, in Honour, distinguish and prefer that of your own Country.

Here my Master concluded his Lecture upon Religion; which was the first I had heard from him upon that Subject, so plain and intelligible. He had often given me little Hints before; which either thro' my want of Capacity, or his, designed Obscurity in speaking, made little or no Impression upon me. But in this last Lesson he had opened his Mind with such an Air of Tenderness and Concern, that everything he said had its due Weight, and sunk deep into my Mind. The more I thought of it, the more I was convinced of the Truth of his Discourse; and every Reflection which arose from it gave me a new and secret Pleasure. The Complacence and Elevation of Spirit which I felt upon believing myself the Son of Hermes vanished; or rather was extinguished, like a lesser Light, by the bright Flame of Truth. A Knowledge, certain and demonstrable, that the Generality of the World were wrong in this Respect, and I, young as I was, free from the Error, gave me a solid and durable Satisfaction, which lasted the whole time of my Life. I was sensible that the Account my Mother had given me of my Birth, was either a plausible Invention of her own to conceal a Truth not proper for her to mention, or that Neanthus had by this Trick first obtained, and since continued, to possess her Embraces. But whether me herself had whispered this Secret to a female Friend whom me trusted, or the Same of my Wit and Learning made my Countrymen conceive something of me more than Mortal; they looked upon me as the Son of that God some time before my Death, and after it bestowed Immortality and divine Honours upon me. However I kept Melidoras Secret, and my own Sense of it entirely to myself; I regarded Neanthus as my real Father, and loved him with a pious and grateful Affection; such indeed as his Fondness and paternal Care of me justly claimed. For his Father Chrysander dying soon after, and leaving him Heir to a good Estate and much Treasure, he generously settled upon my Mother the Farm and Gardens which she rented, and made her a Present of two Talents of Gold.

But my Mind was so wholly engaged in the Pursuit of Knowledge, that I found little Enjoyment out of the Company of my Master Eleutherius, and he was as much charmed with my Parts, and ready Disposition for Learning. The rest of the Youths, my Schoolfellows, were so intent upon Sports and Plays, that they had the utmost Aversion for his dry Philosophy (as they called it) and took advantage of all the Festivals and Times of Solemnity to absent themselves. Then it was that I had the most free and easy Access to his Instructions, and heard him dictate without Reserve. It would have been hard to determine whether the Master expounded, or the Scholar attended, with most Pleasure. One Day, when he had been holding a copious Discourse upon our favourite Topic, Religion, and been exposing, with his usual Clearness and Strength of Reason, the great Inconveniences that had and might proceed proceed from Multitudes possessed with Superstition, and artfully inflamed by wicked designing Priests, he confirmed it with averring, that the more plain and natural any Religion was, the better it would be for the Public, and the more pleasing to God. For (says he) if Mankind would but entertain those just Notions of the Maker of the World, which their own Reason, his faithful Interpreter, would tell them, and resolve not to be imposed upon by Fables and Traditions; 'tis certain that the Religion flowing from thence must be acceptable to God, and beneficial to Mankind. For first, What is more reasonable and more consistent with the Attributes and Honour of God, than to conclude that he expects nothing from his Creatures, but what he has given them Capacities to perform? If we think him to be a God of Justice, we are sure he can require no more. When therefore the Priests, who declare themselves to be the Keepers of his Mysteries and his Will, in one place pretend that he ought to be worshipped with in another, that he expects Wine; in a third, Sheep and Oxen; and that here in our City he is delighted to see his Temple made a public Rendezvous for lewd Women; who (if such Devotion will produce it) bid fair indeed for eternal Happiness, by taking care never to miss the stated Times of Worship, and mortifying their Bodies by a continual Prostitution: Which of these Prescriptions are we to follow as the only right and infallible one? If we ask our Reason; none. If we ask the Priest; he will tell us, that which belongs to his particular God. And as many Religions as there are, so many hundred thousand Priests will ever the same. What must be done then in this uncertain Labyrinth, where there are so many different Ways, and none appears to be (nor certainly is) the right one? Why let us have Recourse to our Reason, that excellent Part of us, by which our Maker has distinguished us from the rest of his Creatures, and try what Information we can get from thence. And that tells us, that, as God is the Perfection of all Good, we can never do better than when we endeavour to imitate, and be like him: By doing as little Hurt, and as much Benefit as we can to our Fellow-Creatures: By keeping our Consciences clear and innocent from evil Designs and Intentions, and forming new Resolutions of proceeding in the Ways of Virtue. Is there any Absurdity in this? Will this make God angry at any time? Nay rather, will it not always please him? If he were to speak to us in the Voice of a Man, and tell us his Will in Words, would he make it any other than this? Could he indeed contrive anything better? And yet how plain, how natural, how obvious to all Mankind is this? Secondly, As this cannot but please God, so nothing can be more beneficial to Mankind. For of what Profit or Use to the World is the great Variety of Rites and Ceremonies which every Nation in it claims? Do they contribute to the Trade of the Country where they are exercised, or to the Strength and Defence of it, or are they in any degree honourable, advantageous or pleasurable to its Inhabitants? If they are, they ought to be retained for the Good of the Public; if not, how ridiculous, nay often how dangerous, is it to keep them up, and let them grow into Custom? What Cruelties do the Kings of Assyria commit in forcing the Nations which they conquer to worship after their Manner? How obstinate are many of those Nations, in choosing rather to endure the sharpest Tortures, than to relinquish the vain Superstitions in which they have been educated? With what a lowering evil Eye do the Priestesses of our Venus behold those chaste Men and Women, who will not suffer their Minds and Bodies to be debauched with the abominable Lusts of *Paphos*? By their libidinous Gestures, and loose Investives, endeavouring to irritate and provoke their lustfully zealous Votaries against them; branding them with the odious Appellations of cold, impotent, or barren; persecuting them with all manner of Obscenities; and declaring that they ought by wholesome Severities, such as Whipping and Hanging, to be forced into an Inclination to do Honour and Service to their Goddess. On the contrary, the Priests who serve Cybele, Joves Mother, must be qualified for it at the Expense of their Manhood; and when they are carrying that old Goddess about the Streets, take an Opportunity to rob all they meet; for when begging is made a Part of Religion, it is reckoned Profane to refuse to give. Now, are not all these as well great Inconveniences to the Public, as mighty ridiculous in themselves? How much better would it be for those miserable People whom the Assyrians take in War, if they had no such barbarous Custom as burning them upon their Altars? What Cruelty, Rancour, Revenge, and Hardness of Heart does this express? Are these Qualities agreeable to the Attributes of God? No surely. Or is it for the public Emolument that such Tempers and Habits of Mind should be encouraged? No: but the contrary is certain. Do the wanton Rites of Venus, practised in this City, in any sense promote public Good? Do they rectify the Mind, or invigorate the Body? Do they make those that stickle for them more Healthy or more Wise? or in any particular contribute to their Well-being? No: but are evidently the Occasion of much Detriment to the Commonwealth in general, as well as very pernicious to private Families. How many Children of both Sexes are initiated into the Mysteries of the Goddess by the Examples of their wanton Mothers? How many Wives, under Pretence of Devotion, take their Fill of surreptitious Loves, and adulterate their Husband's Race with a spurious Issue? Arts and Arms, the Bulwark and Ornament of Cities, are neglected for these baser foster Diversions; and the Women, whom Nature has designed for keeping up our Species, whom he has formed fair and tempting with a thousand agreeable Graces, de feat the End of their Institution by being too liberal of their Charms. They please the Eye, like a Valley of Corn smiling with a vernal Bloom: But when we look to fee a full Harvest, behold! The Clouds overshadow it, the Drops fall thick into the, Furrows; and instead of an impregnating Shower, it overflows with a Deluge of Rain. But every Nation his its religious Rites, and consequently its Follies and Inconveniences of some Kind or other. For tho some of these are indifferent, and innocent enough in themselves, yet through Abuse they may become dangerous to a Community. Such I mean as by a too long Continuance are grown into Custom, and from thence esteemed by the Vulgar as essential, important and necessary Parts of Religion. If the Decency, or perhaps Grandeur with which Religion ought to be attended, in populous Cities especially, requires a sufficient Quantity of Pomp and Show; this should be as changeable as the Fashions of our Dress; that the People might be pleased as well with the Variety and Newness, as Magnificence of them; and the Magistrate have it in his Power, if Reasons of State should require it, to alter as easily as to continue them. How indecent is it to fee the Priests of Pan running naked about the Streets exposing themselves to the Women and Virgins in a Manner too immodest even to be thought on? Yet if the State should attempt to abolish this vile Ceremony, what a tumultuous Outcry would immediately be raised, by the Women especially? who think they shall never feel a Mother's Joys, till they have had a Stroke from these frantic Gesticulators. But as these were all certainly of human Institution, to serve some political End, let us ask our Reason whether God ever told it that he expects any thing of that Kind? It tells us he cannot, and that we should think him a very strange God, if we thought he did. Is there any Ceremony equal to thinking justly of God? Is there any Rite or Custom, though ever so venerable for its Antiquity and Solemnity, so necessary, so truly religious, so agreeable to God, as a Series of virtuous Additions? No: It would be the most stupid Profaneness to suspect, it. How then came the one to be preferred before the other, or even to take place at all in the Minds of reasonable Creatures? How came they to imagine, that a Prejudice in Favour of a Parcel of idle Tricks, would atone for the Suspension of their Reason and the Intermission of their Virtue? For a bigotted Attention to Toys of this Kind makes us, for a Time, lose the Assistance of those two noble Guides. Why, my Æthalides, as great a Riddle as this seems to be, it is easily accounted for: Those who have the Advantage of Reason, could never act thus, un less that were first blinded and perverted. If People, in Pursuance of the Dictates of that excellent Faculty, were to exercise themselves in Habits of Virtue only, and resist these ridiculous Fopperies, what Occasion would there be for Priests? Therefore this Set of Men, to prove the Necessity and to enhance the Dignity of their Office, pretend that the Gods themselves have ordained and commanded these Things, and appointed them Administrators and Executors of their Will. They know that there is a Consciousness of Duty in every Man's Heart, which tells him that he ought to endeavour after Virtue, and lets him see there is a Pleasure in doing Good; but fills his Mind with Shame and Remorse upon committing an ill Action, and makes him afraid to neglect doing that which is right. This natural Fear the Arch Priests work upon and improve by their own Impostures; and, among the vulgar ordinary People, find it no very difficult Task. The Balance of a Man's Reason, when he comes deliberately to weigh his own Actions, will incline him to believe, that according as they have tended to Virtue or Vice in this Life, he shall meet with Punishments or Rewards in the

Shades below. And as the Generality of Mankind leans more toward Vice than Virtue, and must consequently be often agitated with this Fear; by this Means there is Room for the designing Priest to step in and bias their Judgment; which is commonly done, by flattering their Hopes, and lessening their Fears, He comforts and encourages their drooping Spirits, by assuring them the Gods may be appeased and reconciled by something else besides Virtue: That such a Thing as an Hecatomb of Bullocks may go a great way; that building of a Temple, and dedicating it to some particular God, will do well; and that settling a good Revenue for the Maintenance of the Priests that must belong to it, is most effectual Thus People who are conscious of having committed Injuries among Men, and solicitous how they shall escape the Lash of the Furies, are very willing to believe those that find out Expedients for their Security, though ever so absurd and unreasonable. We have neglected (say they) to imitate the Attributes of God, in being Just and Good; but will He be pleased with Immolations and Victims? Will the Blood of Bulls and Goats and Sheep entertain him so much, that he will overlook our Injustice for their Sakes, and commute our Punishment for the Slaughter of Beasts? If he will, we are ready to satisfy his Demands, even to the one Half of our Dilates: And how venerable, how sacred, how useful an Order of Men are these Priests, his Attendants and Interpreters, who tell us these good Tidings, and can effect such glorious Things for us!

To think thus, my, Æthalides, is natural to a Mind disturbed and perverted by Fear; but Thou seest how far it is from the Dictates of cool Reason and consequently how far from being agreeable to the divine Nature. Behold Pandicæus, who neither enters our profaned Temples, nor attends at our abominable Rites; how chearful, how calm, how undisturbed is his Mind? how healthy and vigorous his body? how unreprovable all his

Actions? He walks through the Streets, and, with an unconcerned failing Countenance, sees the Entrails crackling and frying upon the Altars, He salutes the High-Priest with a well-bred Civility, and puts on an outward Gravity when lie talks with him; but laughs inwardly at the Farce he is acting, and admire, at the Stupidity of Mankind. The Deity, whom they so grossly make Court to, as if he had the Appetites and Passions of a Mortal, Pandicæus contemplates with the Light of his Reason, and studies to imitate by the Practice of Justice, Benignity, and all kind of social Virtues. His Heart tells him, that this is the Duty of a reasonable Creature; his constant Exercise of it has made it habitual; and the uninterrupted Pleasure which flows from such a Rectitude of Thoughts and Actions, confirms him in his Opinion, that what is thus good and joyful must be Godlike.

For, what ill-natured Deities, my Æthalides, are the Gods represented to be, when we are told that we cannot please them unless we torment ourselves? Justice and Temperance, Honesty and Sobriety, Complaisance and Good-Will, are exceeding pleasant and delightful, as well as useful and advantageous to that Society in which they are practised: But Fear, Superstition, Moroseness, Passion, Suspicion, Jealousy and Vain-Glory, which are the Ingredient. of most People's Religion, are tormenting to ones self, and troublesome to others. Which of these Qualities is most likely to please God, the good-natured or the ill natured? It needs no Answer.

Thus, from time to time, did this wife judicious Man sow the Seeds of Knowledge in my Heart, and inoculate the Buds of Virtue in my Mind. I had a Memory which happily retained the Things committed to it; and though the Food with which I was supplied, might well be thought too strong for one of such tender. Years, yet I had an Understanding that could digest it, and turn it into the most wholesome Nourishment. I was scarce arrived to the twelfth Year of my Age, when I was admired and caressed by all that saw me: By the graver Sort for my Learning and Knowledge; by the Young, the Spritely and the Gay, for my Wit and Beauty. As much as I was seasoned and fortified against the Attacks of Vanity, from the wife Instructions of my Master, I could not, without being touched with a secret Pleasure, perceive the Eyes of the admiring City turned upon me as I passed along. They courted me into their Houses with Importunity; and there was a visible Emulation among them about gaining my Esteem by the Delicacy of their Entertainments.

But in all these, there was none whose Fondness was expressed with so much Ardor, and even Impetuosity, as that of Iphigenia a Matron of the first Rank; and who surpassed the rest of my Admirers in Munificence, as much as in the Excess of her Love, and the Superiority of her Condition. She bound a Bracelet of Pearl many times round my left Arm, and fastened on Gems of great Price for the Buttons of my Sandals. She retained me with the tenderest Blandishments; and the sensible Tokens she continually gave of the Reality of her Kindness, disposed me to return the Affection, by devoting to her Service those Intermissions of Leisure, which are such necessary Reliefs to Study. Yet I could not discover which was most the Object of her Passion, the Turn of my Mind or Body; she seemed to be in Raptures upon the Contemplation of either of them; but when I was speaking in the most engaging Manner, would frequently break her Attention to my Discourse by reiterated Kisses, and convulsive Embraces. She obtained leave of my Mother, that I should stay whole Nights in her House; and Melidora from a Sense of the Obligations laid on her by so noble a Lady, contented herself sometimes a Week together without seeing me.

To the Breast of Eleutherius I committed all my Secrets. He was become rather a Friend than a Master, and was as sincere in assisting me with his Counsel now, as before he had been diligent in furnishing me with his Instructions. To him I communicated every new Motion in this amicable Affair, and modeled my Behaviour according to his Opinion. He considered that Iphigenia was past that Age in which the Levities and Sallies of Youth plead Excuse for unruly Passions, and the Consequences which they produce: That tho' her Husband had long since been indifferent to her, she avoided giving him any designed Offence; as knowing that notwithstanding her Charms were not capable of affecting him now, he would have raged with Jealousy at the Thoughts of another's possessing them. But Eleutherius perceived that her Fondness for me was so far from alarming him, that he had rather encouraged and given in to it, and from thence concluded, that, thinking his Honour safe, he did not intend to deprive his Wife of so innocent a Pleasure as she seemed to enjoy in a Boy's Company. He thought too, that Iphigenia would compound by such an Indulgence for all the severe Restraints her Affectations of Virtue had imposed upon her; and that all the little Efforts of Desire, which for a long time she had checked and concealed, would break out with united Forces, and center in her Passion for me. From these Observations he formed a most artful Scheme for my future Conduct; in which it was contrived how I might converse with Iphigenia, without diminishing her Love and the Advantages flowing from it, the good Opinion of her Husband, or my own Integrity. She was wealthy beyond Account, and most of her Riches being superadded to her Dowry by the Death of great Relations, remained in her own Disposal. She gave me every Day fresh Testimonies of her Affection, by repeated Instances of her Liberality. I was distinguished in my Apparel as if I had been her own Son, and she often carried me with her to the Temples, and among the Assemblies of honourable Women; where I encountered such a Variety of odd Adventures, as gave Occasion to many entertaining and instructive Discourses of Eleutherius. Religion, Gallantry, Politics, and Trade, were the Topics I was required to be most observant upon: These were the Supplies by which our private Discourses were from time to time kept up which, by occasional Excursions I took care to provide for the Repast of my retired Preceptor, whose Age and Station hindered him from mingling in the Chase, and being a present Spectator of the Sport. Various were the Mazes I trod in tracing the different Intrigues of Lovers, Statesmen, Priests and Artificers. Affectations, Impostures, and pernicious Designs of what Kind soever were the Marks I aimed at; and my Haunts were contrived to be in those Places where these were most likely to be found. Of which an Account will be given in this History in Order as they happened.

FINIS